Ripley's Believe It or Not!

Developed and produced by Ripley Publishing Ltd

This edition published and distributed by:

Mason Crest
370 Reed Road, Broomall, Pennsylvania 19008
www.masoncrest.com

Printed and bound in the United States of America.

First printing
9 8 7 6 5 4 3 2 1

Ripley's Believe It or Not!
Eating Habits
ISBN-13: 978-1-4222-2567-7 (hardcover)
ISBN-13: 978-1-4222-9242-6 (e-book)
Ripley's Believe It or Not!—Complete 16 Title Series
ISBN-13 978-1-4222-2560-8

Library of Congress Cataloging-in-Publication Data

Eating habits.
     p. cm. – (Ripley's believe it or not!)
ISBN 978-1-4222-2567-7 (hardcover) – ISBN 978-1-4222-2560-8 (series hardcover) –
ISBN 978-1-4222-9242-6 (ebook)
 1. Food–Miscellanea–Juvenile literature. 2. Food habits–Miscellanea–Juvenile
literature. 3. Curiosities and wonders–Juvenile literature. I. Title: Eating habits.
TX355.S394 2013
641.3–dc23
                              2012020339

PUBLISHER'S NOTE
While every effort has been made to verify the accuracy of the entries in this book, the
Publisher's cannot be held responsible for any errors contained in the work. They would
be glad to receive any information from readers.

WARNING
Some of the stunts and activities in this book are undertaken by experts and should not
be attempted by anyone without adequate training and supervision.

Disbelief and Shock!

EATING HABITS

www.MasonCrest.com

EATING HABITS

Fantastic food. Get a taste of the world's most

bizarre eating habits when you open up this book.

Read about bottles of snake wine, the BBQ the size

of a football field, and the snake that ate

a fully grown wallaby!

In Bubblegum Alley in San Luis Obispo, California, this face is made entirely of bubblegum.

Ripley's research

WHY DOES SODA EXPLODE?

There is some dispute over what actually causes carbonated drinks to explode when candy is dropped into the bottle, but most scientists agree that it is a reaction between the carbon dioxide gas in the liquid and the mints. The mints dissolve the surface tension around the individual bubbles of carbon dioxide gas, allowing the bubbles to gather together on the candy. Soon the liquid cannot contain the gas any longer and it explodes out of the top of the bottle. Diet soda works better than regular soda, but nobody knows exactly why.

Soda Shower

In Leuven, Belgium, students donned ponchos and braved a sticky deluge when they simultaneously dropped mints into 1,360 bottles of diet cola and watched as the drink exploded high into the air.

Potato Peacock

This colorful 8-ft-tall (2.4-m) peacock-shaped lantern made of potatoes appeared at a department store in Shenyang, China, in January 2008. The vegetables were finely sliced until translucent and then arranged so that multi-colored lights shone through.

EXCLUSIVE POTATO ■ An exclusive French potato can sell for $800 per kilo. Only 100 tons of the La Bonnotte variety are cultivated each year and it is grown only on the island of Noirmoutier, off the west coast of France, where the fields are fertilized with nothing but seaweed.

FISH LUNCH ■ A retired couple from England have traveled 60 mi (96 km) for a fish-and-chip lunch at their favorite seaside resort every day for the past ten years. Cypriot-born Ermis and Androniki Nicholas have visited Weston-super-Mare, Somerset, over 2,600 times, journeying around 160,000 mi (257,495 km) and spending almost £20,000 (about $32,000) on fish and chips.

SNAKE VODKA ■ Texan rattlesnake rancher Bayou Bob Popplewell has been selling bottles of vodka containing dead baby rattlers as a healing tonic. He uses the cheapest vodka he can find as a preservative for the snakes and compares the end result to cough syrup.

CHEESE CHANTS ■ An Austrian school for dairy farmers has won a string of prizes for its Grottenhofer Auslese cheese since it began playing Gregorian chants to the cheese while it matures. The head of the school believes the monks' music stimulates the micro-organisms that help the cheese mature.

MIGHTY MEATBALL ■ Gary Travis, owner of Meatball Mike's restaurant in Cranston, Rhode Island, made a pork-and-beef meatball weighing 72 lb 9 oz (33 kg) in August 2008.

GENEROUS GESTURE ■ Eighty-eight-year-old Golda Bechal of London, England, bequeathed the bulk of her estate—more than $20 million—to the owners of her favorite Chinese food restaurant.

HEAVY POTATO ■ A potato grown on the Isle of Man, off the western coast of England, weighed 7 lb 13 oz (3.5 kg)—the weight of a healthy newborn baby.

OUTSIZE EGG ■ In 2008, Titi, a one-year-old hen belonging to the Martinez-Guerra family in Campo Florido, Cuba, laid an egg weighing a colossal 6.34 oz (180 g)—nearly three times the weight of the average hen's egg.

FRY MUSEUM ■ The Belgian city of Bruges has opened a museum dedicated to French fries. The brainchild of Eddy Van Belle, the Frietmuseum chronicles the history of the nation's favorite food from its conception in the 1700s, along with a collection of fry art, a display of the fry in cartoons, and an exhibition of kitchen fryers.

COLA CRAVING ■ A Croatian man has drunk nothing but Coca-Cola for more than 40 years. Pero Ajtman of Karanac is now in his seventies and has been drinking up to five glasses of Coke a day since 1968 when he promised his mother he would never touch alcohol. He says he is in perfect health and is happy to drink Coke until the day he dies.

Ripley's ask

How did you start carving watermelons?

I was inspired to learn the art of fruit carving when I saw a watermelon sculpture at a Tokyo hotel that was holding a festival celebrating Thai culture. Watermelons have a large area to carve and are stronger than other fruits.

What tools do you use to carve them?

Only one knife—a carving knife made in the Kingdom of Thailand.

What is your favorite watermelon carving?

It is the Japanese crane and tortoise, which are symbols of good fortune.

How long does it take to carve a watermelon?

It takes around 90 minutes.

What happens to your carved fruit?

After appreciating the carvings, we chill them and eat them.

How long do the carvings last?

At room temperature in an exhibition, they last two days. In a refrigerator, they can last for two weeks.

Watermelon Marvels!

Japanese food sculptor Takashi Itoh has been carving amazing art in watermelons for seven years. Entirely self-taught, he became an expert in just three weeks. His carvings include dragons, slogans, and Japanese cranes and tortoises. According to Takashi, you can carve many different fruits and vegetables—as well as watermelons, he recommends using papayas, pumpkins, carrots, and Japanese radishes.

EXPENSIVE WATER ■ There is a type of water that sells for nearly $17 an ounce. Kona Nigari water—a desalinated water rich in minerals from the deep seas off Hawaii—is much prized by the Japanese and is sold in concentrated form to be mixed with regular water.

DIVAN INTERVENTION ■ There is a new restaurant in New York where customers eat on king-size beds. Created by Sabina Belkin, Duvet is furnished with beds, pillows, and sheets instead of tables, chairs, and tablecloths.

FARMERS' REVENGE ■ In some parts of the world, humans have taken revenge on crop-destroying locusts by turning them into a tasty delicacy—usually deep-frying them or covering them in chocolate.

BALL OF CORN ■ A popcorn ball 24 ft 6 in (7.5 m) in circumference and weighing 3,415 lb (1,550 kg) was manufactured in Lake Forest, Illinois, in 2006.

TOMATO CANNERS ■ California is by far the largest producer of processed tomatoes in the United States. California's prolific canners process more tomatoes in a few days than Ohio, the second-largest producing state, processes during the entire season.

TOMBSTONE TEA ■ The New Lucky Restaurant in Ahmadabad, India, is built around, and over, a centuries-old Muslim cemetery—with the graves located in the café floor between the dining tables. The shin-high graves are painted green, have candles on top of them and every day the restaurant manager decorates each one with a single dried flower.

STRETCHED SKEWER ■ In 2007, students in Cyberjaya, Malaysia, prepared a kebab that weighed 8,377 lb (3,800 kg) and was more than 1¼ mi (2 km) long.

FRUIT SALAD ■ In 2008, around 400 people from Swan Hill, Victoria, Australia, sliced and diced locally grown nectarines, plums, peaches, melons and grapes to create a fruit salad that weighed a whopping 6.2 tons. The finished salad was loaded into a giant fruit bowl on January 25 and then eaten the next day, Australia Day.

CAMEL SPIT ■ Chef Christian Falco from Perpignan, France, spit-roasted a 1,210-lb (550-kg) camel for 15 hours at Safi, Morocco, in November 2007. He used almost 3 tons of wood and 32 pt (15 l) of oil to cook the camel, which was big enough to feed 500 people.

CRÊPE TOWER ■ In 2008, Gus Kazakos of Ocean City, New Jersey, made a French crêpe tower that stood 3 ft 4 in (102 cm) tall, weighed around 300 lb (136 kg), and consisted of 510 individual crêpes. He used 120 lb (54 kg) of flour, 140 eggs, 170 pt (80 l) of milk, 80 lb (36 kg) of chocolate, 40 lb (18 kg) of bananas, and 40 lb (18 kg) of strawberries to make his edible tower and could have gone higher had the chocolate not started to melt, risking the possible collapse of the entire structure.

SWEET DREAMS ■ The Northwest Fudge Factory of Levack, Ontario, Canada, made a slab of fudge 45 ft 6 in (13.8 m) long, weighing 5,038 lb (2,285 kg), in 2007.

HEART ATTACK GRILL ■ The Heart Attack Grill at Chandler, Arizona, prides itself in offering potentially unhealthy meals, ranging in size from the "Single Bypass Burger" to the monster "Quadruple Bypass Burger"—all served with "Flatliner Fries," which it promises are deep-fried in pure lard. Fittingly, the restaurant's waitresses are dressed as nurses.

PLUMP PIZZA ■ In 1987, at Havana, Florida, Lorenzo Amato and Louis Piancone cooked a pizza that weighed a whopping 44,457 lb (20,165 kg) and was later cut into more than 94,000 slices.

RODENT REMEDY ■ For over 40 years, Jiang Musheng of China has eaten live tree frogs and rats to ward off abdominal pains.

SUPER SUNDAE ■ In 1988, Mike Rogiani of Edmonton, Alberta, Canada, created a mammoth ice-cream sundae that weighed 54,917 lb (24,909 kg) and was so big it had to be mixed in an empty swimming pool.

BEEFY BAKE ■ In 2000, the Denby Dale Pie Company of West Yorkshire, England, baked a meat-and-potato pie that was 40 ft (12 m) long and weighed 26,455 lb (12,000 kg).

A SPOONFUL OF SAND ■ Ram Rati of Lucknow, India, eats 1 lb (454 g) of sand every day to fight stomach complaints.

BURGER ADDICT ■ Don Gorske of Fond du Lac, Wisconsin, has eaten more than 23,000 Big Macs in the last 36 years. To prove his addiction, he keeps all the sales receipts in a box and says the only day he didn't eat a Big Mac was the day his mother died.

CHICKEN FEED ■ Jan Csovary from Prievidza, Slovakia, eats chicken for breakfast, lunch, and tea, and has consumed over 12,000 chickens since the early 1970s.

EGGS-CEPTIONAL ■ In 2002, the Lung Association of Brockville, Ontario, Canada, produced an omelette weighing 6,510 lb (2,953 kg) from 60,000 eggs.

NOTHING BUT CHEESE ■ Dave Nunley from Cambridgeshire, England, has eaten nothing but grated mild Cheddar cheese for over 25 years and goes through 238 lb (108 kg) of it every year.

WIGGLY FEAST ■ Wayne Fauser from Sydney, Australia, regularly eats live earthworms, either in sandwiches or just plain.

CHOCOLATE-COVERED SALAD ■ Danny Partner of Los Angeles, California, used to eat 12 iceberg lettuces covered in chocolate sauce every day.

LARGE O'LANTERN ■ In 2007, farmers in Cullinan, Pretoria, South Africa, made a pumpkin pie 27 ft (8.2 m) long and weighing 2,534 lb (1,150 kg).

DAILY GRAZING ■ Gangaram from Kanpur, India, eats 2 lb (907 g) of grass every day because he says it gives him energy.

CARROT CRUNCHER ■ Julie Tori from Hampshire, England, has eaten at least 4 lb (1.8 kg) of carrots every day for over ten years. On the one day she didn't have her favorite vegetable, she was seized by a panic attack.

CELEBRATION CAKE ■ To celebrate the centennial of Las Vegas, Nevada, in 2005, chefs made a birthday cake 102 ft (31 m) long that weighed 130,000 lb (59,000 kg).

STING SPREAD ■ Father-of-two Hasip Kaya of Turkey has been addicted to eating live scorpions since he was a boy.

FLY FEAST ■ In protest at his town's garbage collection service, a man named Farook from Tirunelveli, India, started eating nothing but flies.

WHAT A PICKLE ■ Using 58,000 cabbage heads, 2,200 cooks in Seoul, South Korea, in 2008, prepared a dish of kimchi—spicy pickled cabbage—that weighed 315,261 lb (143,000 kg).

MANTIS ON THE MENU

Tofu garnished with spring onion and a generous helping of praying mantis is on the menu at the home of alternative chef Shoichi Uchiyama, from Tokyo, Japan, who collects insects from around his home. He advises that deep frying is the best way to cook them, and thinks that school children should be taught the benefits of eating creepy crawlies, as they are plentiful and nutritious.

QUICK MIX ■ In Las Vegas, Nevada, in February 2008, bartender Bobby Gleason mixed 253 cocktails in an hour, averaging just over four cocktails a minute.

HALF-MILE SAUSAGE ■ In July 2008, the village of Graus in northern Spain prepared a sausage that was more than half a mile (0.8 km) long. It was made from 1.2 tons of pork and was cooked using 1,323 lb (600 kg) of charcoal.

BATMAN SOUP ■ The Toy and Action Figure Museum at Pauls Valley, Oklahoma, houses an exhibit of unusual food products related to comic books and superheroes. Items include such culinary oddities as Superman Pasteurized Process Imitation Cheese Spread, Spiderman Cookies, and Batman Soup.

UPSCALE CANDY ■ Lebanese chocolatier Patchi created boxes of chocolates that went on sale at Harrods department store in London, England, for $10,000 each. The 49 chocolates, which were made from organic cocoa, rested on suede and were separated by gold and platinum linings. In addition, each one was decorated with gold and a Swarovski crystal flower or handmade silk rose. The boxes themselves were personalized for the buyer and wrapped with leather and handmade silk.

CANDY BOWL ■ U.S. rock band Van Halen had it written into their contract that at every concert they played they were to be provided backstage with a bowl of M&M's®—but with the specific instructions that they were to have all the brown candies removed.

LOBSTER LOVERS ■ A 22-lb (10-kg) male lobster named Big Dee-Dee was rescued from the pot after becoming a popular tourist attraction in Shediac, New Brunswick, Canada. The monster lobster, believed to be over 100 years old, was caught in July 2008. More than 1,000 tourists a day visited the fish market to see him, prompting Laura-Leah Shaw of Vancouver, British Columbia, and two anonymous organizations in Ontario to pay $3,000 to buy him and put him back in the sea.

MARS MAD ■ Keith Sorrell of Liverpool, England, has eaten nothing but his favorite chocolate bar for more than 17 years. Every day he eats at least a dozen Mars Bars, which combine chocolate, nougat, and caramel, in place of meals.

SPACE YOGURT ■ A Japanese dairy has been selling space yogurt, made using two types of lactic acid bacteria that spent 10 days in space aboard a Russian Soyuz rocket. Half of the bacteria died inside the rocket, but the strong, surviving bacteria are said to give space yogurt a more full-bodied flavor than that made with standard earthbound bacteria.

cheesy Politicians

Working eight hours a day for a week in a 40-degree cooler, Wisconsin artist Troy Landwehr carved his own version of John Trumbull's historic painting *Declaration of Independence*—from 2,000 lb (907 kg) of Cheddar cheese.

EATING HABITS

Ripley's—
Believe It or Not!®

M&M® Eminem

Mexican artist Enrique Ramos made this 40 x 30 in (100 x 76 cm) portrait of rapper Eminem from over 1,000 M&M's® candies.

YOUNG STAFF ■ All the food at the Kinderkookkafe in Amsterdam, the Netherlands, is cooked and served by children. In fact, no adults are allowed to eat there unless they have been invited by a child.

BACON-FLAVORED CHOCOLATE
■ Chicago chocolatier Katrina Markoff creates unusual-flavored bars of candy, including curry and chocolate and chocolate with mushrooms. Her company's latest offering, Mo's Bacon Bar, which contains chunks of smoked bacon combined with milk chocolate, sold out within 48 hours when it went on sale at Selfridge's department store in London, England, in November 2008.

CHEESE MITES ■ The manufacture of Milbenkäse, a variety of German cheese, includes the intentional introduction of cheese mites. The mites look like crumbs on the cheese's rind.

EATS EYELASHES ■ In Brazil, there is a species of cockroach that eats eyelashes, usually those of young children while they are asleep.

RAMPANT RATS ■ A plague of rats ate the entire rice crop in India's northeastern state of Mizoram during 2007 and 2008, despite millions of the rodents being killed after the government paid a bounty of two rupees per rat-tail.

TOP BANANA ■ Broadview Heights, Ohio, disk jockey Ross Cline peeled and ate five bananas in one minute in March 2008.

CHAMPAGNE DELIVERY ■ When guests on the beach at the Cap Maison Hotel on the Caribbean island of St. Lucia want to order champagne, they raise a red flag and the drink is then delivered to them by zip-wire.

CHILI BUG ■ New research from the University of Washington has revealed that bugs are responsible for the heat in chili peppers. The spiciness is a defense mechanism developed by some peppers to combat a microbial fungus that invades through punctures made in the outer skin by insects. If unchallenged, the fungus would destroy the plant's seeds before they could be eaten by birds and widely dispersed.

EASTER EXTRAVAGANZA ■ A decorated Easter egg, measuring 48 ft 6 in (14.8 m) long and 27 ft 6 in (8.4 m) in diameter, was created in Alcochete, Portugal, in 2008.

GARLIC MENU ■ Garlic's Restaurant in London, Ontario, Canada, has a menu with the emphasis on garlic, offering such dishes as garlic ice cream and garlic cloves dipped in chocolate, which can be washed down with garlic martinis.

ROBOT BARTENDER ■ A Japanese beer maker has devised a robot bartender, Mr. Asahi, who can serve customers with a smile in less than two minutes. Mr. Asahi, who weighs a quarter of a ton, can pull pints, and open bottles and pour them for customers. He works behind a specially designed bar and can politely respond to questions via an operator-controlled system that includes more than 500 vocal effects.

DRIED SAFFRON ■ It takes between 50,000 and 75,000 saffron crocus flowers to make just 1 lb (450 g) of dried saffron spice—that's the equivalent of an entire football field of flowers.

LOBSTER OMELET ■ An omelet at the Le Parker Meridien restaurant in New York sells for $1,000. It contains 10 oz (280 g) of sevruga caviar, a whole lobster, and six eggs.

VORACIOUS APPETITE ■ A locust can eat its own weight—0.07 oz (2 g)—in plants each day. This means that just a very small part of an average swarm of locusts eats the same amount of food in one day as 10 elephants or 2,500 humans.

L·O·C·U·S·T

A swarm of pink locusts engulfed a beach on the Spanish Canary Island of Fuerteventura in November 2004. Vacationers hurriedly evacuated the area when the locusts arrived. The creatures had been severely battered during their ocean crossing and many arrived with broken legs and wings, dying shortly after landing. They were part of a swarm of more than 100 million locusts that flew in from western Africa in the course of one weekend. One swarm in Morocco was 145 mi (230 km) long and 500 ft (150 m) wide and contained an estimated 69 billion locusts. The insects' numbers were boosted that year by areas of the Western Sahara receiving 100 times more rainfall than usual, creating conditions that were ideal for locust breeding.

Ripley's
Believe It or Not!

GREAT LOCUST PLAGUES

1915 From March to October, a plague of locusts stripped areas in and around Palestine of almost all vegetation.

1954–55 A swarm of locusts in Kenya covered more than 385 sq mi (1,000 sq km), contained 40,000 million insects, and weighed 88,000 tons.

1958 Ethiopia lost 167,000 tons of grain to locusts, enough to feed a million people for a year.

1987–89 A plague of locusts that originated in Sudan spread as far as India, affecting 28 countries and costing around $300 million to treat an area of 100,000 sq mi (260,000 sq km).

2000 100 billion locusts swarmed in Australia, affecting 11,500 sq mi (30,000 sq km) in South Australia. They turned the sky so black that outback weather stations gave false readings of heavy rain.

2004 Locust swarms necessitated the spending of $400 million to treat an area of 50,000 sq mi (130,000 sq km) in 20 countries. Harvest losses were valued at $2.5 billion.

2005 Hundreds of thousands of locusts invaded southern France, devouring everything from farmers' crops to flowers in village window boxes.

SWARM

Wobbly Building

St. Paul's Cathedral was molded from jelly for the Architectural Jelly Design Competition 2008 at University College London, where professional architects entered sweet structures including an airport and a bridge. The orange-and-mango-flavored cathedral was created by jelly makers Bompas and Parr, who use architectural techniques in their jelly molds. Entries were judged on their wobbling qualities amid the sound of wobbling jelly piped through the building.

BUTTER SCULPTURE ■ For the Harrisburg, Pennsylvania, Farm Show in 2008, Jim Victor created a sculpture from 1,000 lb (453 kg) of butter. The sculpture—a take on "Mary Had a Little Lamb"—depicted a girl trying to take her cow on a school bus.

EDIBLE MENU ■ The menu at Moto restaurant in Chicago, Illinois, is edible. Chef Homaru Cantu loaded a modified ink-jet printer containing mixtures of fruits and vegetables and then printed tasty images downloaded from the Internet onto edible sheets of soy bean and potato starch. Customers can even flavor their soups by ripping up the menu and adding it to their dish.

Dough Art

Food-artist Prudence Emma Staite celebrated the city of Rome at the launch of a well-known pizza chain's new pizzeria at the Museum of London, England, in 2007. She constructed the Colosseum, the head of Pope Benedict XVI, and the Spanish Steps all from pizza dough.

EDIBLE RACE ■ An edible boat race was staged in Eyemouth, Scotland, in 2008, where 30 competitors sent such vessels as an apple raft with a cabbage-leaf sail out to sea. The winner was a chocolate tart, although the most seaworthy was judged to be a coracle of slow-baked lasagne sheets. Some entries, notably melon-skin boats, were disqualified for not being entirely edible.

CHOCOLATE ROOM ■ As part of a Valentine's Day promotion in 2008, a Belgian chocolatier unveiled a room in Manhattan that was made entirely from chocolate—including the walls, furniture, artwork, chandelier, fireplace logs, and candles.

CANDY CASTLE ■ In Zagreb, Croatia, in 2008, Krunoslav Budiselic spent 24 hours building a 10-ton chocolate castle from around 100,000 chocolate bars. The finished candy construction stood 10 ft (3 m) high on a chocolate base that measured 20 x 7 ft (6 x 2.1 m). Afterward, the individual chocolate "'bricks" were sold off for charity.

GLOBAL EGG ■ In 2008, a hen in Zaozhuang City, China, laid an egg with a pattern on it that resembled a map of the world. The four oceans, Greenland, and the Hainan Islands in the South China Sea were all distinctly recognizable.

ROYAL MAC ■ Royal accounts revealed in 2008 that Queen Elizabeth II owns a drive-through McDonald's burger restaurant. A retail park in Slough, visible from the Queen's State Apartments at Windsor Castle, Berkshire, England, was recently purchased by the Crown for $184 million and it includes a McDonald's.

BACON FLOSS ■ Seattle-based novelty dealer Archie McPhee has introduced a new line in dental floss—one that has the flavor of crispy bacon. The company already sells bacon-scented air freshener.

SERIAL EATER ■ In April 2008, New Yorker Timothy Janus ate 141 pieces of nigiri sushi in just six minutes. He has also devoured 4 lb (1.8 kg) of tiramisu in six minutes and 10 lb 8 oz (4.8 kg) of noodles in eight minutes.

NANO NOODLES ■ Japanese scientists have created a bowl of noodles so tiny that it can be seen only through a microscope. Students at the University of Tokyo carved the bowl, which has a diameter of just one-25,000th of an inch, from microscopic carbon nanotubes. The noodles inside the bowl measured one-12,500th of an inch in length and were only one-1.25 millionth of an inch thick.

EXOTIC ICES ■ In 2008, the city of Yokohama celebrated the 130th anniversary of the arrival of ice cream in Japan with a festival showcasing such regional flavors as raw horse, curry, octopus, garlic, prawn, chicken wings, cheese, beer, eel, beef tongue, and pit viper.

PIZZA RUSH ■ A Domino's pizza in Gulfport, Mississippi, sold 7,637 pizzas in a single day in August 2008, customers being enticed by the offer of 10-in (25-cm) pepperoni pizzas for just $2 each.

LARGE BLUEBERRY ■ A 12-year-old boy from New York State has grown what is believed to be America's biggest blueberry. Zachary Wightman from Kerhonkson exhibited his 0.24-oz (6.8-g) fruit at the Ulster County Fair in July 2008.

BLUE BREAD ■ Dozens of Australian shoppers were alarmed in 2008 when they put their supermarket-bought garlic bread in the oven to cook—and it turned blue. The mystified manufacturers promptly recalled the bread and blamed the problem on an old batch of garlic.

PORK STAMP ■ To mark 2007 being the Year of the Pig, China released a scratch-and-sniff stamp that smelled like sweet-and-sour pork—and the glue on the back of the stamp was even flavored like the popular dish.

HOT CURRY ■ In 2008, chef Vivek Singh from The Cinnamon Club restaurant in London, England, produced a lamb-based curry containing some of the world's hottest chilies, including Dorset Naga and Scotch Bonnet. The end result was so hot that, before eating it, customers had to sign a disclaimer saying they were aware of the nature and risks involved with tasting the curry.

FIRE-EATER

Inspired by a fantasy role-playing game, Misty Doty of Washington State commissioned a masterpiece of a cake in the form of a dragon for her husband John. The tasty creature was made by expert cake-maker Mike McCarey of Redmond, Washington, from chocolate and vanilla with a chocolate buttercream filling. It took 12 hours to complete.

Sticker Art

Barry Snyder of Erie, Colorado, creates 4-ft-sq (0.4-sq-m) mosaic artworks using stickers from store-bought fruits and vegetables. An average mosaic takes him around six months to create and uses 4,000 colorful stickers, many of which are sent to him by friends from around the world. His work is so sought-after that an original can sell for around $10,000.

BURGER BRIDES ■ Three couples were married on Valentine's Day 2008 at the same burger restaurant in Columbus, Ohio. Flower girls threw salt and pepper packets and the cake resembled three burgers with fries and a drink.

SECRET RECIPE ■ A hotel in England's Lake District asked guests and kitchen staff to sign a secrecy clause to protect its recipe for sticky toffee pudding after a couple tried to post it on the Internet. The closely guarded recipe has been locked in a vault at the Sharrow Bay Hotel for over 40 years and only a handful of people have ever been taught how to make the dish.

MECHANICAL EATING ■ At Michael Mack's 's Baggers restaurant in Nuremberg, Germany, no humans serve the customers. Instead, orders are taken by customers pressing touch-screen computers and the food is delivered mechanically in little pots on wheels riding on long metal tracks that run from the kitchen to the tables.

NO LIGHTS ■ At O. Noir restaurant in Montreal, Quebec, Canada, customers dine in total darkness. There are no lights, no candles, and all cell phones and glowing watches must be removed.

PUNCH BOWL ■ At an extravagant party during the reign of Britain's King William III (1688–1702), the Honorable Edward Russell used the fountain in his garden as a giant punch bowl for mixing drinks. The ingredients included 560 gal (2,120 l) of brandy, 1300 lb (590 kg) of sugar, 25,000 lemons, 20 gal (75 l) of lime juice, and 5 lb (2.2 kg) of nutmeg. Russell's butler rowed around the fountain in a small boat, filling the punch cups for the guests.

CORNDOG CHOMP ■ No fewer than 8,400 people ate corndogs simultaneously at the Iowa State Fair in Des Moines in August 2008.

Humongous Burger

Brad Sciullo of Uniontown, Pennsylvania, managed to eat his way through a 15-lb (6.8-kg) burger—but it took him 4 hours and 39 minutes. The monster burger—the Beer Barrel Belly Bruiser—was prepared by Denny's Beer Barrel Pub of Clearfield, Pennsylvania, and when toppings and the bun were added, it weighed a whopping 20 lb (9 kg).

MEAT FEAST

More than 30,000 people devoured 61,600 lb (27,940 kg) of meat—that's 2 lb (1 kg) for each person—at a giant barbecue near Asunción, Paraguay, in 2008. The fires covered an area the size of a football field.

BEAN DIET ■ Neil King from Essex, England, lost 140 lb (63.5 kg) in nine months—by eating six cans of baked beans every day. Eating beans for breakfast, lunch, and dinner, he devoured more than 1,500 cans or half a ton of beans and saw his weight drop from 420 lb (190 kg) to less than 280 lb (127 kg).

PANCAKE FEAST ■ The Fargo, North Dakota, Kiwanis Club made nearly 35,000 pancakes in eight hours at its Pancake Karnival in February 2008. The pancakes were served with more than 1,100 bottles of syrup.

DOGGIE BEER ■ A Dutch pet-shop owner has created a new beer—for dogs. Gerrie Berendsen, from Zelhem, has persuaded a local brewery to launch a nonalcoholic, beef-flavored brew called Kwispelbier, which is Dutch for "tail-wagging beer."

EEL DRINK ■ A new energy-boosting drink has gone on sale in Japan—made from eels. The fizzy, yellow-colored drink contains extracts from the heads and bones of eels along with five vitamins that are contained in the fish.

GIANT CHEESECAKE ■ In June 2008, bakers at Eli's Cheesecake World in Chicago created a 2,000-lb (907-kg), three-tiered cheesecake made from 1,330 lb (603 kg) of cream cheese, 300 lb (136 kg) of sugar, 150 dozen eggs, 100 lb (45 kg) of butter cream frosting, and 100 lb (45 kg) of marzipan.

BURNED FOOD ■ Harpist Deborah Henson-Conant from Arlington, Massachusetts, runs the online Museum of Burnt Food, dedicated to "accidentally carbonized culinary masterpieces." She started the museum in the late 1980s and her exhibits include inadvertently cremated quiches, pizzas, and baked potatoes.

FIERY CHILI ■ Created by vegetable grower Michael Michaud from Dorset, England, the Dorset Naga chili is so hot that cooks are advised to wear gloves at all times when preparing it in order to avoid skin irritation. An extract of the Dorset Naga needs to be diluted in water 1.6 million times before any trace of its heat disappears and it therefore racks up 1.6 million Scoville Units—the measure of chili heat—compared to Tabasco sauce's mere 8,000.

HORNET SALIVA ■ The saliva of Japan's giant hornet is a component in a Japanese sports drink said to reduce muscle fatigue.

Sea-horse Kebabs
Fried sea-horses were among the delicacies sold at markets in Beijing, China, for the 2008 Olympic Games.

BUSY DINER ■ A restaurant in Damascus, Syria, can serve more than 6,000 customers simultaneously. The Damascus Gate Restaurant has a staff of 1,800, a kitchen of 26,900 sq ft (2,500 sq m), and a dining area of 581,250 sq ft (54,000 sq m).

CHEESE WHEEL ■ A wheel of cheese weighing 1,590 lb (721 kg)—that's more than the weight of eight fully grown men—was produced by a factory in Altay, Russia, in 2008.

HAM-BUSH FOILED ■ Caught in the act of stealing meat from the freezer of a restaurant in Gloucester, Massachusetts, a thief tried to beat off owner Joe Scola by hitting him over the head with 5 lb (2.2 kg) of frozen prosciutto. However, Scola sent the would-be thief running for cover by whacking him in the face with a ham first.

UDDER LUXURY ■ Dairy cows at a farm in the Netherlands have been receiving V.I.P. treatment in the hope they will produce better-tasting milk. Nancy Vermeer's 80 cows are pampered with massages and get to lie on soft rubber mattresses sprinkled with sawdust and even water beds.

TUNA ACUPUNCTURE ■ For superior sushi, a Japanese company administers acupuncture to each tuna fish prior to its death, in order to reduce the amount of stress it suffers.

MOOSE MEAT ■ In December 2006, Swedish astronaut Christer Fuglesang became the first person to take dehydrated moose meat into space.

ONION GENES ■ It may be a humble vegetable, but an onion's genetic code is nearly six times longer than a human's.

Crunchy Crawlies
The Japanese have put a creepy-crawly twist on their traditional sushi by adding large and spiky insects. The dish is not for the squeamish, and includes caterpillars, spiders, moth larvae, cockroaches, and cicadas on a bed of sushi rice.

NO WASTE ■ Le Spirite Lounge in Montreal, Quebec, Canada, is a vegan restaurant with two strict rules: first, everyone must finish their meal in order to get a dessert; and, second, unless they finish their dessert, they can never return to eat at the restaurant again.

ALCOHOLIC FERMENT ■ People with auto brewery syndrome can become spontaneously drunk when, amazingly, their body ferments normal food into alcohol during the process of digestion.

LUXURY BURGER ■ After six months of development, Burger King® launched a $185 burger in London, England, in 2008. Made using ingredients from seven countries, from Japan to France, The Burger, which is the size of a regular Whopper, combines Japanese beef with white truffles, Cristal Champagne onion straws, Pata Negra ham drizzled in Modena balsamic vinegar, organic white wine and shallot-infused mayonnaise, and pink Himalayan rock salt, all served up in an Iranian saffron and truffle bun.

PIZZA CHAIN ■ In May 2008, Scott Van Duzer and employees of Big Apple Pizza and Pasta in Fort Pierce, Florida, created a chain of pizzas 722 ft (220 m) long.

KANGAROO BURGERS ■ An Australian scientist has recommended that eating kangaroo burgers could help save the planet. Dr. George Wilson says sheep and cows produce more methane gas emissions through flatulence than kangaroos, whose digestive systems produce virtually no greenhouse gas emissions at all.

FRIED SPIDER

Near the town of Skuon, Cambodia, a species of tarantula spider is bred in holes in the ground specifically for food. The spiders are fried until the legs are stiff and the abdomen is not too runny, giving a crispy exterior and soft center said to resemble the taste of chicken. The spiders sell for 500 riel (12 cents) each and their popularity as a foodstuff is thought to stem from the regime of the Khmer Rouge (1975–79), when hunger forced people to eat spiders to survive.

JAW-DROPPING

A monster Amethystine python, thought to be over 16 ft (4.9 m) long, swallowed a fully grown wallaby and her joey in February 2008. Darren Cleland encountered the creature on the banks of the Barron River, west of Cairns, Australia, and said, "We figured if it could eat the wallaby, it could easily eat our 5-year-old."

Ripley's research

HOW DO PYTHONS SWALLOW SUCH BIG PREY?

Unlike most animals, the jaws of a python are loosely connected to the skull with elastic ligaments, allowing them to open wide to an angle of 180 degrees. The lower jaw is separated into two and unconnected at the chin, so that it can break apart sideways. This means that, amazingly, pythons can swallow prey ten times the size of their mouths.

Pythons wrap their bodies around their prey until it suffocates. As it can take hours for a snake to consume a large animal, they can extend their windpipe beyond the mouth to ensure they can still breathe. Pythons need to eat only once every few weeks, depending on the size of the meal, and they have the rare ability of being able to digest all the bones.

Pythons can open their jaws to such dimensions that a greedy specimen can swallow amazingly large prey relatively easily. This snake wouldn't have to eat again for weeks.

SERPENT SNACK ■ The body of a 32-year-old man from Mindoro Island in the Philippines was recovered inside a 23-ft (7-m) python in 1998.

DOG FOOD ■ An Australian family watched as a 16-ft (4.8-m) python swallowed their pet Chihuahua in front of them in February 2008.

DEADLY BATTLE ■ A 13-ft (4-m) python exploded after trying to swallow a 6-ft-6-in (2-m) alligator in the Florida Everglades in 2005.

HEADFIRST ■ In 2003, a 10-ft (3-m) python in Rangamati, Bangladesh, swallowed a 38-year-old woman up to her waist until local villagers beat it to death.

SWALLOWED WHOLE ■ A 20-ft (6-m) African rock python swallowed a 10-year-old boy in Durban, South Africa, in 2002.

WRONG MOVE ■ A 2-ft-7-in (80-cm) carpet python swallowed four golf balls in Australia after mistaking them for chicken eggs. The balls were safely removed by surgery.

BELLY ACHE ■ An 18-ft (5.5-m) python got into trouble when it swallowed an entire pregnant sheep in Malaysia in 2006. Afterward, it was too full to move and firefighters were called in to move it off the road.

STOMACH SIGNALS ■ A python measuring 22 ft 9 in (7 m) swallowed a 51-lb (23-kg) Malaysian Sun Bear in Malaysia. The bear was being electronically tracked and when it didn't move for four hours scientists became concerned. They retrieved the radio collar in a surgical operation and let the snake go.

HORROR SQUEEZE ■ Twenty-nine-year-old Ee Heng Chun was partially swallowed headfirst by a 308-lb (140-kg) python in Malaysia in 1995. The python was scared off and shot by police.

HOT MEAL ■ A 12-ft (3.6-m) Burmese python needed surgery after it swallowed an entire queen-size electric blanket—with the electrical cord and control box still attached. The blanket was in the cage so that the 60-lb (27-kg) snake could keep warm.

DOGGIE SNACK ■ A man from Merced, California, got a shock when he returned home to find both his snake and dog missing, before discovering his 200-lb (91-kg) Burmese python with a bulge in its stomach about the size of his 30-lb (14-kg) Pit Bull Terrier. The massive reptile escaped from its cage, swallowed the dog and then hid under the house while it digested its meal.

Australian Darren Cleland was alerted by his neighbor's dog to the incredible scene of a 16-ft (4.9-m) python wrapping its elastic jaws around a full-size wallaby and its baby joey. Wallabies can grow to a length of 2 ft 7 in (80 cm)—not including the tail—and weigh up to 44 lb (20 kg).

A TASTE FOR TOMATO

Guinness Rishi from Delhi, India, is always striving to achieve unique feats. Recently he finished off a bottle of tomato ketchup in less than 40 seconds. In 2001, Rishi personally delivered a pizza from Delhi to the Ripley's Believe It or Not! museum in San Francisco, California.

EATING HABITS

www.ripleys.com

BUSY CHEF ■ Working alone, Donnie Rush of Bay St. Louis, Mississippi, made 142 pizzas in a single hour in August 2008.

PORTLY PATTY ■ A 115-lb (52-kg) sausage patty—big enough to serve more than 450 people—was made in Hatfield Township, Pennsylvania, in February 2008. The huge patty, which was 6 ft (1.8 m) in diameter and 1½ in (3.8 cm) thick, was cooked over 160 lb (72.5 kg) of charcoal for about 40 minutes. It took several people to flip it halfway through cooking.

DEATH DINER ■ A death-themed restaurant has opened in Truskavets, Ukraine—housed in a 65-ft (20-m) windowless coffin. The brainchild of funeral parlor director Stepan Pyrianyk, the restaurant, called Eternity, takes the form of a huge casket decorated with dozens of wreaths and smaller coffins.

CRUSTY MAYO ■ Spanish chefs have devised a new method of making mayonnaise from colloidal silicon dioxide—the substance that comprises 60 percent of the Earth's crust. They have also created a nutritious sausage from the leftovers from dragnet fishing, roasted prawns in beach sand, and designed edible plates made from wheat, rice and maize.

MEATY COLOGNE ■ Burger King™ made a novel Christmas gift in 2008—a men's cologne called Flame, which smells of barbecued meat.

CANDY MURAL ■ More than 4,000 office workers used a quarter of a million Smarties—colored chocolate candies—to create a 500-sq-ft (46-sq-m) mural depicting major London landmarks, including the Big Ben tower, the London Eye, and Wembley Stadium.

TWO-FOOT SCONE ■ Bakery shop owner Helen Hallett and her family from Torquay, Devon, England, created a scone that weighed 57 lb (26 kg) and measured 2 ft (60 cm) in diameter. The colossal cake was made from a 100-year-old recipe and it included 22 pt (10.4 l) of clotted cream. At 700 times bigger than a standard scone, it had to be baked in a mold specially constructed by welders.

JAIL BAIT ■ The Jail restaurant in Taiwan has been designed to resemble a prison. Customers enter via a big metal door and are greeted by staff wearing prison uniforms. Handcuffed, the guests are then led to their cell, which is complete with metal floor, rusty iron bars on the window, and sliding prison door.

Spaghetti Contest

It was forks at the ready as competitors furiously tucked into bowls of pasta at a spaghetti-eating competition held at a festival in Sydney, Australia, that celebrated all things Italian.

THE 134-POUNDER ■ In 2008, Mallie's Sports Grill & Bar of Southgate, Michigan, created a giant burger weighing 134 lb (61 kg). The 24-in (60-cm) burger needed three men using two steel sheets to flip it and went on the menu at a price of $399.

LONG CHOPSTICKS ■ The Marco Polo Hotel in Dubai, United Arab Emirates, has manufactured a pair of chopsticks that are 22½ ft (6.85 m) long—that's equal to the size of the tallest pair of stilts!

CAFÉ CHAOS ■ Two women were rushed to hospital with burning sensations in their mouths in July 2007 after a café in Queenstown, New Zealand, mistakenly served dishwashing detergent as mulled wine.

TEQUILA BOTTLES ■ Since he started his collection in 1994, Ricardo Ampudia from Tepoztlan, Mexico, has amassed more than 3,600 tequila bottles, including over 500 different brands. His oldest bottle dates back over 100 years, while his most expensive—made of pure gold poured over hand-blown glass—is worth $150,000. He also has a 3-ft-long (90-cm) tequila bottle in the shape of a rifle and another containing the tail of a rattlesnake.

ANGER RELEASE ■ Customers at Isdaan restaurant in the Philippines can release their anger by throwing cups, saucers, plates, even working TV sets, at a wall.

CHOCOLATE CREATIONS

It's hard to imagine wanting to consume the incredible works of art produced by Jean Zaun of Lebanon, Pennsylvania, even though they are made out of chocolate, sugar, and food-coloring. Jean worked as a candy coater in the family confectionery business, but now makes edible copies of famous works of art and eerily lifelike three-dimensional reproductions, including a pair of boots worn by Vincent van Gogh and a white-chocolate deer skull with antlers that look remarkably real.

Deer Skull

This piece was part of a three-dimensional still life for a wedding reception that looked like a forest floor. Jean used a real deer skull and then added white chocolate for the head and antlers.

CHOCOLATE BACON ■ There's a new snack on sale at the Santa Cruz Boardwalk seaside amusement park in California—chocolate-covered bacon. The unusual combination was created by fourth-generation candy-maker Joseph Marini III in the belief that most people love bacon and most people also love chocolate.

108 VARIETIES ■ A restaurant in Mindoro, Wisconsin, serves more than 100 different types of burger. Located on Highway 108, Top Dawg's, run by Paul and Sue Kast, offers 108 burgers on its menu, including the Ginza Burger (made with teriyaki sauce and water chestnuts). The owners are even printing T-shirts for those who can eat their way through all 108—not in one sitting!

CRAB CAKE ■ Chef Fred Bohn of Dover, Delaware, spent nine hours cooking a giant crab cake that weighed in at 235 lb (106.5 kg). The crab cake was cooked in a 3-ft (90-cm) rotisserie-style pan and was later divided into 600 crab sandwiches.

SEEING DOUBLE ■ A restaurant in Yiwu, China, is run by two couples in which both the man and the woman of one couple is the identical twin of the man and the woman in the other. The twin brothers married the twin sisters in 2005, leading to confusion for their customers, who could not understand how the same couple could work for 21 hours every day.

WINE-TASTING ■ In May 2008, the British pub chain J.D. Wetherspoon conducted a synchronized wine-tasting in its inns across the U.K.—and 17,540 people turned up to drink a free glass of Coldwater Creek Chardonnay.

LUCKY TIP ■ In February 2008, a customer presented a racehorse, named Mailman Express, to 71-year-old waitress A.D. Carrol of Houston, Texas, to thank her for good service.

SHARP COOKIE ■ Fifteen-year-old Girl Scout Jennifer Sharpe from Dearborn, Michigan, sold 17,328 boxes of her scout group's signature cookies in 2008 by setting up shop daily on a street corner.

Van Gogh's Boots

These boots are based on a pair depicted in one of Van Gogh's paintings. Jean used a pair of worn work boots as molds, welding the parts together with dark chocolate.

SUPER GRAPES ■ The Kagaya Inn at Ishikawa, Japan, sells grapes the size of table tennis balls for $26 each. The tomato-colored Ruby Roman grapes, which have been under development since 1994 in a state-led project, are so sought after that a single bunch—containing around 35 grapes—sold for $910 in August 2008.

DATE PLATE ■ In July 2008, organizers of the Liwa Date Festival at Abu Dhabi in the United Arab Emirates displayed a vast plate piled with 4,410 lb (2,000 kg) of dates. The oval-shaped steel plate, which was fitted with 15 carrying handles, measured 33 x 6½ ft (10 x 2 m).

BABY RICE ■ Naruo Ono, owner of Yoshimiya, a rice shop in Fukuoka, Japan, sells baby-shaped bags of rice that proud parents can send to friends and relatives as birth announcements. The bags, known as Dakigokochi, are custom made to feature the newborn's face and to weigh the exact amount as the baby.

BRIDAL CAKE ■ After ten years of marriage, Chidi and Innocent Ogbuta of Dallas, Texas, renewed their vows in style—accompanied by a 5-ft (1.5-m) wedding cake made into a life-size model of Chidi in her bridal dress. The $6,000 butterscotch cake took five weeks to create and was made from 2 gal (7.5 l) of amaretto liqueur, 50 lb (23 kg) of sugar, and 200 eggs. The cake bride's dress was made of icing and the head and arms were of polymer clay. The end result weighed a whopping 400 lb (180 kg) and it needed four men to lift it into the wedding venue.

HAPPY MEAL ■ Mother-of-two Juliet Lee from Germantown, Maryland, can eat seven chicken wings, 1 lb (450 g) of nachos, three hot dogs, two pizzas, and three Italian ice creams in just over seven minutes.

BEEF BARBECUE ■ Around 1,250 people grilled 26,400 lb (12,000 kg) of beef in Montevideo, Uruguay, in April 2008. The grill was nearly one mile long and firefighters lit more than six tons of charcoal to barbecue the beef.

TEARLESS ONION ■ Scientists from New Zealand and Japan have created an onion that doesn't make you cry when you cut it. Using gene-silencing technology, they managed to insert DNA into onions, creating a sequence that switches off the tear-inducing gene in the onion so that it doesn't produce the enzyme that makes us cry.

CHOCOLATE FERRARI ■ A full-size Ferrari Formula One car was unveiled in Italy in 2008—made entirely from chocolate. Confectioners spent more than a year making the $24,000 car out of 4,405 lb (2,000 kg) of Belgian chocolate, but at a Ferrari-owners' club party in Sorrento it was smashed up with hammers and handed out to guests who took bits home in bags.

BEER BATH ■ At the Chodovar Beer Spa in the Czech Republic, guests take soothing, hot, 20-minute baths in dark beer. The beer yeast is believed to be beneficial to the skin.

BLACK MARKET ■ A single black watermelon fetched $6,100 at an auction in Japan in August 2008. The sought-after 17-lb (7.7-kg) premium Densuke watermelon—grown on the northern island of Hokkaido—was one of just 65 from the first harvest of the season.

SCOTCH EGG ■ A London, England, hotel chef created a huge Scotch egg that weighed 13 lb 10 oz (6.2 kg). Lee Streeton prepared the dish from an ostrich egg weighing 3 lb 12 oz (1.7 kg), sausage meat, haggis, and breadcrumbs. The egg alone took an hour and a half to boil and the entire cooking process took eight hours.

BIG BOX ■ British chocolatier Thorntons unveiled a box of chocolates in London's Leicester Square in April 2008 that weighed 4,805 lb (2,180 kg). The giant box was 16 ft 6 in (5 m) high, 11 ft 6 in (3.5 m) wide and contained more than 222,000 chocolates.

LATE SUPPER ■ A Canadian couple cashed their coupon for a free dinner at a Canton, Ohio, restaurant—15 years after receiving it. For its grand opening in 1993, Nicky's Restaurant had released balloons with cards attached offering a free dinner for two. One of the balloons sailed across Lake Erie and landed in the backyard of Margaret and Ken Savory in Waterford, Ontario, but ill health prevented them from taking up the offer until August 2008.

gum wall

Watch out for the alleyway entirely covered in chewed bubblegum next time you are in San Luis Obispo, California. The gum plastered to the brickwork in Bubblegum Alley has been spreading since the late 1950s. Additions have built up over the years and include a bright red face made from the sticky stuff. Visitors are welcome to add to the collection and some even sample some of the secondhand gum on offer.

EATING HABITS

www.ripleys.com

This red gum face is one of the more artistic offerings in the alley.

While most of the gum on the walls lost its taste and color long ago, there are still fresh submissions every day, if you have the stomach for it.

Glazed Gator

The annual Explorers Club Dinner in New York is renowned for the bizarre delicacies it offers to guests. Along with glazed and oven-roasted alligator, diners have enjoyed honey-glazed tarantula, mealworms, housefly larvae, and rattlesnake.

RAT MEAT ■ An Indian welfare minister has advised people to farm rats for food as a way of beating rising prices. Poor people in parts of India have traditionally eaten rats that they hunted in paddy fields, but Vijay Prakesh says rich people should also sample rat meat, which he claims is full of protein and tastes even better than chicken.

PRISON FOOD ■ Convicted murderers staff a luxury Italian restaurant that is located behind walls 60 ft (18 m) high inside the 500-year-old top security Volterra Prison in Tuscany, Italy. The chefs, waiters, and even the pianist are all inmates, and every customer has to undergo strict security checks.

HEAVENLY FEAST ■ Phuljharia Kunwar, an 80-year-old widow from Bihar, India, spent $37,500 on a two-day feast for 100,000 villagers in 2008 in the hope that her display of generosity would please the gods and secure a place for her in heaven.

VAMPIRE CAFÉ ■ A restaurant in Tokyo, Japan, has a vampire theme. The Vampire Café is decorated with blood-red walls, as well as skulls, crosses, and black coffins dripping with red candle wax. Many of the dishes are served in a similar style, including a Dracula dessert that comes with crucifix biscuits.

SPEEDY SANDWICH ■ Mexican caterers prepared a "torta" sandwich 144 ft (44 m) in length in just five minutes at Mexico City in 2008. The quick-fire sandwich, each section of which had a different flavor, weighed a staggering 1,320 lb (600 kg) and contained 30 ingredients. It featured thousands of pieces of bread, lettuce, onion, and tomato mixed with hundreds of gallons of mayonnaise, mustard, and spicy sauces.

FOOD COLLECTION ■ Volunteers for the Greater Toronto Apartment Association knocked on more than 160,000 apartment doors in the Canadian city in a single day in April 2008 to solicit food donations—and collected more than 262,500 lb (119,000 kg) of canned and packaged food for charitable causes.

BEER COFFIN ■ Chicago's Bill Bramanti has had a coffin specially built to resemble a huge can of his favorite beer. The 67-year-old paid $2,000 to have the casket painted blue and red like his beloved Pabst Blue Ribbon beer and, in the hope that he won't be needing it for a while yet, he has filled it with beer and ice and is using it as a cooler.

INDOOR STORMS ■ At a restaurant in San Francisco, customers eat against a backdrop of occasional light tropical rainstorms, complete with thunder and lightning—which all take place indoors! The Tonga Room's Polynesian theme extends to the dance floor, which is built from the remains of a lumber schooner that once traveled regularly between the city and the South Sea Islands.

FISH DINNER ■ On May 30, 2008, organizers of the sixth annual Polish Heritage Festival served up 2,552 fried fish dinners at the Hamburg Fairgrounds, New York State.

300 CHEFS ■ The West Lake restaurant in Changsha, Hunan Province, China, employs 1,000 people (including 300 chefs) and seats 5,000 customers.

ASPARAGUS SPEARS ■ Joey Chestnut of San Jose, California, ate 8 lb 13 oz (4 kg) of deep-fried asparagus spears in 10 minutes at the Stockton Asparagus Festival, California, in April 2008.

Not just a pest but a gourmet meal, raw rat meat waits to be cooked at a restaurant in Taiwan, which has been serving up the rodent on a plate for decades. Cooked in herb-infused stews and soups, and deep-fried, the chef assures customers that the rats are not from the sewers, but local fields and farms.

LEMONADE CUP ■ Arthur Greeno, owner of a Tulsa, Oklahoma, branch of Chick-fil-A, made a 839-gal (3,815-l) cup of lemonade in August 2008. To make the drink, 11,730 lemons were hand-squeezed, yielding 145 gal (660 l) of lemon juice, which was added to more than 1,000 lb (453 kg) of sugar, 250 lb (113 kg) of ice, and 580 gal (2,640 l) of water. In 2007, he had made a 131-gal (595-l) hand-spun milkshake.

PRINGLE BURIAL ■ Fredric J. Baur, the designer from Cincinnati, Ohio, who thought up the Pringles tube, was so proud of his invention that he asked to be buried in one. So when he died in May 2008, some of his ashes were placed in a Pringles can that was buried in a grave along with an urn containing the rest of his remains.

CHOCOLATE WRESTLING

Sweet-toothed revelers at a music festival on an island in the Danube River in Budapest, Hungary, let off steam as they wrestled in a pool of chocolate provided by a local confectionery company.

Oyster Fan

On his way to winning an oyster-eating competition in New Orleans, Louisiana, champion gobbler Patrick Bertoletti scoffed an incredible 420 oysters in just eight minutes. The Chicago-based chef has also won jalapeno-pepper and chicken-wing eating competitions.

ELECTRONIC TONGUE ■ Scientists at the Barcelona Institute of Microelectronics in Spain have built an electronic tongue that can determine the variety and vintage of a wine at the press of a button. The handheld device is made up of six sensors that detect characteristic components such as acid, sugar, and alcohol.

SEABED CHAMPAGNE ■ Two hundred bottles of champagne sat on the seabed off Finland for over 80 years before being sold in 2008—for around $300,000 a bottle. The 1907 vintage champagne was en route to the Russian royal family when the ship carrying it sank.

FLAPJACK FLIPPER ■ Canadian TV presenter Bob Blumer, who hosts "Glutton for Punishment" on the Food Network, cooked and flipped 559 flapjacks in one hour at Calgary, Alberta, in July 2008—that's about one every 6.5 seconds.

POTATO CHIPS ■ Bernd Schikora of Vreden, Germany, has a collection of more than 2,000 empty potato chip packets from all over the world, including Europe, the United States, and Asia—and in 2008 they went on display in a cultural history exhibition at a local museum.

RIB MUNCHER ■ Bob Shoudt of Royersford, Pennsylvania, ate 6 lb 13 oz (3 kg) of ribs in 12 minutes in an eating contest at Bridgeport, Connecticut, in August 2008. One competitor was still chewing 10 minutes after the contest had ended, his mouth clogged with rib meat.

MEAL TICKET ■ Takeru Kobayashi from Nagano, Japan, earned $200,000 in prize money and appearance fees from competitive eating in 2007 and has legions of female fans. Showing that he has not lost his appetite for the sport, he devoured 11 lb (5 kg) of chicken satay in 12 minutes in Singapore in July 2008.

FISH ATTRACTION ■ To entertain diners, a restaurant in Changchun, China, has around 20 carp swimming in the 13-ft-long (4-m) urinal in the men's bathroom.

DEPRESSION-ERA PRICES ■ An Italian restaurant in Harlem, New York City, where Frank Sinatra and Tony Bennett were once regulars, marked its 75th anniversary in 2008 by charging 1933 prices. Patsy's Restaurant was selling a 12-oz (340-g) steak and grilled salmon for 90 cents, a slice of pizza for 60 cents, and most beverages for 10 cents.

TWO-TON CAKE ■ In January 2009, 55 cooks from Mexico City spent 60 hours making a two-ton cheesecake, which they cut into 20,000 slices.

WINNING DOG ■ In the patisserie showpiece section of the International Culinary Olympics, held in Erfurt, Germany, in 2008, Michelle Wibowo from West Sussex, England, won gold with a life-sized sugar sculpture of a hound dog. It took her four days and 44 lb (20 kg) of sugar to make the dog, which even had drool.

SNOW BEER ■ Every year Kevin O'Neill, founder of Australia's Snowy Mountains Brewery, collects a bucket or two of the first snow of winter to fall at Charlotte Pass, New South Wales, and adds it to his next batch of beer.

PEARL FIND ■ Raymond Salha and his wife were eating oysters at their restaurant in Tyre, Lebanon, in 2008, when they discovered 26 pearls inside one shell on her plate.

SNAKE WINE

In Vietnam, you can buy snake wine—often with a dead snake preserved inside the bottle. Venomous snakes are usually chosen for the reptilian brew, but because their poison is protein-based, it is inactivated and therefore rendered harmless by the ethanol in the rice wine. The wine is popular because snakes are said to have medicinal qualities, curing everything from poor eyesight to hair loss.

 Index

ACKNOWLEDGMENTS

COVER (t/r) Takashi Itoh, (b/r) Photograph Matt Kuphaldt/Cake created by Mike McCarey of Mike's Amazing Cakes/Commissioned by Misty Doty for John Doty; BACK COVER Greta Ilieva. Jellies by Bompas & Parr; 4 Marya Figueroa; 6–7 Sven Dillen/AFP/Getty Images; 8 CNImaging/Photoshot; 9 Takashi Itoh; 11 Tony McNicol/Rex Features; 12 Reuters/Lucas Jackson; 14–15 Reuters/Juan Medina; 16 (t) Greta Ilieva. Jellies by Bompas & Parr, (b) UPPA/Photoshot; 17 Photograph Matt Kuphaldt/Cake created by Mike McCarey of Mike's Amazing Cakes/Commissioned by Misty Doty for John Doty; 18 (t) Barry Snyder, (b) Logan Cramer III courtesy Denny's Beer Barrel Pub; 19 Sven Dillen/AFP/Getty Images; 20 (t) Cameron Spencer/Getty Images, (b) Tony McNicol/Rex Features; 21 Reuters/Chor Sokunthea; 22–23 Newspix/Rex Features; 24 Niklas Halle'n/Barcroft Media; 25 Reuters/Daniel Munoz; 26 (l) Jean L. Zaun, (r) © steve-photo/fotolia.com; 27 Jean L. Zaun; 29 (t, b) Marya Figueroa 28–29 (dp) Amytha Willard; 30 Esther Dyson via Flickr; 31 (t) Reuters/Nicky Loh, (b) Reuters/Laszlo Balogh; 32 (t) Judi Bottoni/AP/PA Photos, (c) © nata_rass/fotolia.com; 33 Paul Thompson/World Illustrated/Photoshot

Key: t = top, b = bottom, c = center, l = left, r = right, sp = single page, dp = double page

All other photos are from Ripley Entertainment Inc.
Every attempt has been made to acknowledge correctly and contact copyright holders and we apologize in advance for any unintentional errors or omissions, which will be corrected in future editions.